What do you call a bear with no teeth?

A gummy bear.

What is yellow on the outside and grey on the inside?

A school bus full of elephants.

All rights reserved. © Tickles & Giggles 2020.
No part of this book may be: reproduced, stored in any retrieval system, or transmitted in any form or by any means, electronic, manual, photocopying, recording, scanning, or otherwise without express written permission of the copyright owners. Printed in the USA.

This book belongs to

I am awesome.

My one wish is that I can

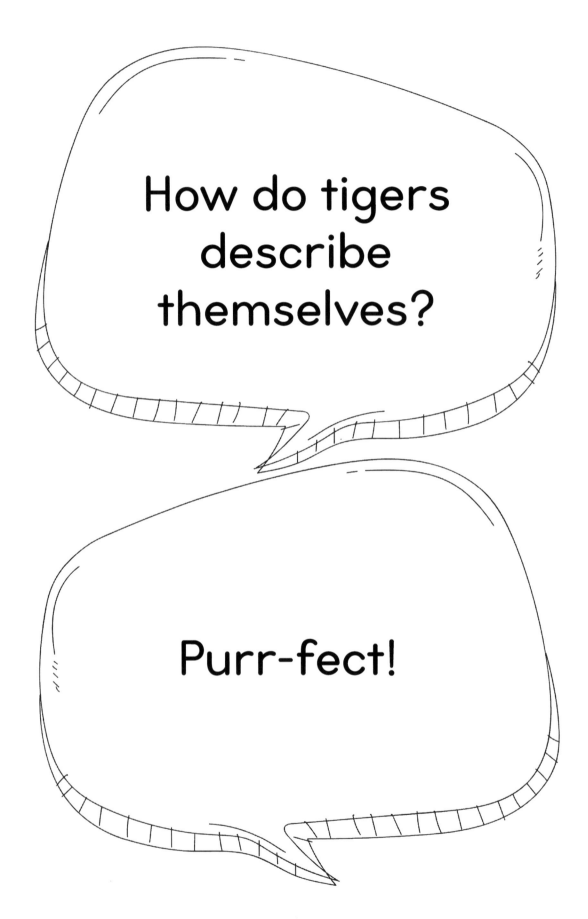

Color by numbers

1 green
2 orange
3 brown
4 blue
5 beige
6 white

Color by numbers

1 green
2 gray
3 brown
4 blue
5 beige
6 white

What game should you never play with an elephant?

Squash!

Color by numbers

1 green
2 gray
3 brown
4 blue
5 yellow

Why does a leopard always lose at hide and seek?

Because he's always spotted.

Color by numbers

1 green
2 orange
3 brown
4 blue
5 yellow

Color by numbers

1 green
2 yellow
4 blue
3 brown

What is black and white, black and white, black and white and green?

Three zebras fighting over a pickle.

Color by numbers

1 green
2 gray
3 brown
4 blue
5 yellow
6 white

Why don't giraffes like to go to the playground?

Because the monkeys use them for slides.

Color by numbers

1 green
2 orange
3 brown
4 blue
5 yellow

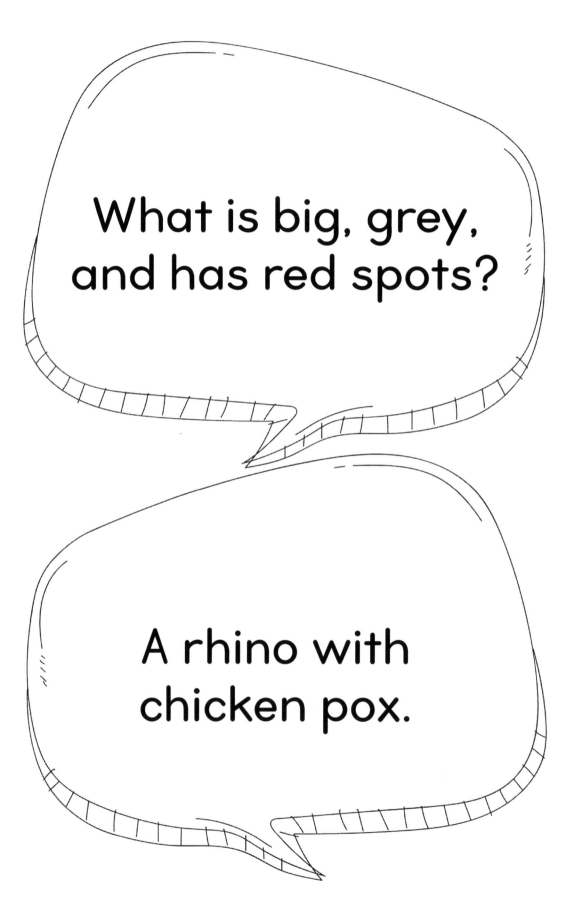

Color by numbers

1 green
2 gray
3 brown
4 blue
5 yellow

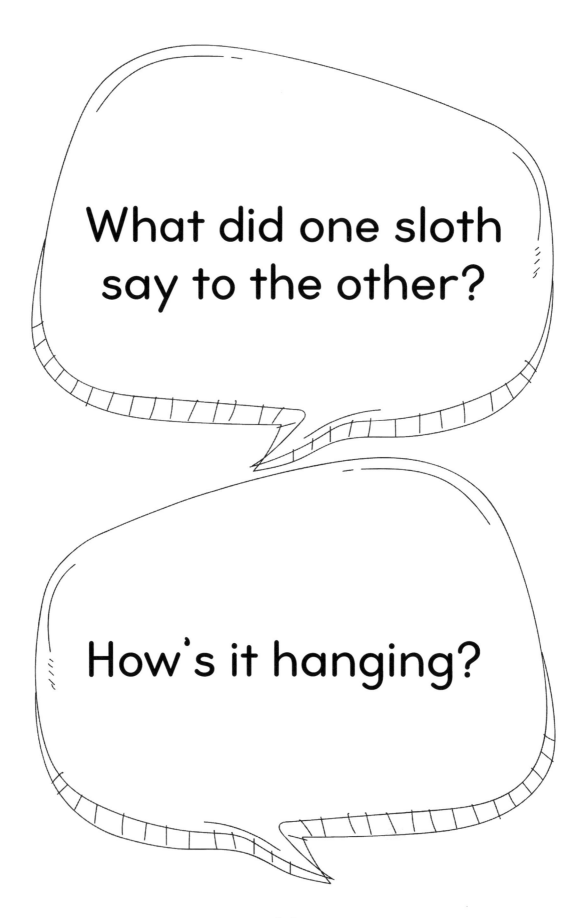

Color by numbers

1 green
2 orange
3 brown
4 blue
5 yellow

What happened when the lion ate the clown?

He felt funny.

Color by numbers

1 green
2 orange
3 brown
4 blue
5 beige
6 yellow

What's an alligator's favorite drink?

Gator-ade.

Color by numbers

1 green   4 blue
2 white   5 yellow
3 brown   6 red

Color by numbers

1 green
2 gray
3 brown
4 blue
5 yellow

Why do tigers have stripes?

So they don't get spotted.

Complete the maze

What has 3 words, 8 letters, is easy to say and hard to prove?

I'm a zebra.

Complete the maze

Why does a giraffe take so long to apologize?

It takes a long time for him to swallow his pride.

Complete the maze

Why did the lion lose the card game?

Because he was playing with a cheetah.

Complete the maze

Why don't alligators like fast food?

It's too hard to catch.

Complete the maze

Complete the maze

Why did the rhino paint her toenails red?

So she could hide in a bowl of cherries.

Complete the maze

What do elephants and trees have in common?

They both have big trunks.

Complete the maze

What is small, furry, and slightly purple?

A koala holding its breath.

Complete the maze

Complete the maze

Complete the maze

Why did the animals wear red tennis shoes?

To hide in the strawberry patch.

Matching game

Matching game

What kind of ant is so strong it can knock down trees?

An elephant.

Matching game

55

Why did the hippo float down the river on its back?

He didn't want to get his tennis shoes wet.

Matching game

57

How do you hunt for elephants?

Hide in a bush and make a noise like a peanut.

Matching game

What do you call a monkey that loves potato chips?

A chipmonk.

Matching game

61

Matching game

63

Why shouldn't you mock an alligator?

It might come back to bite you in the end.

Matching game

65

Why don't you ever see a hippo hiding in a tree?

Because they are good at it.

How many?

How many?

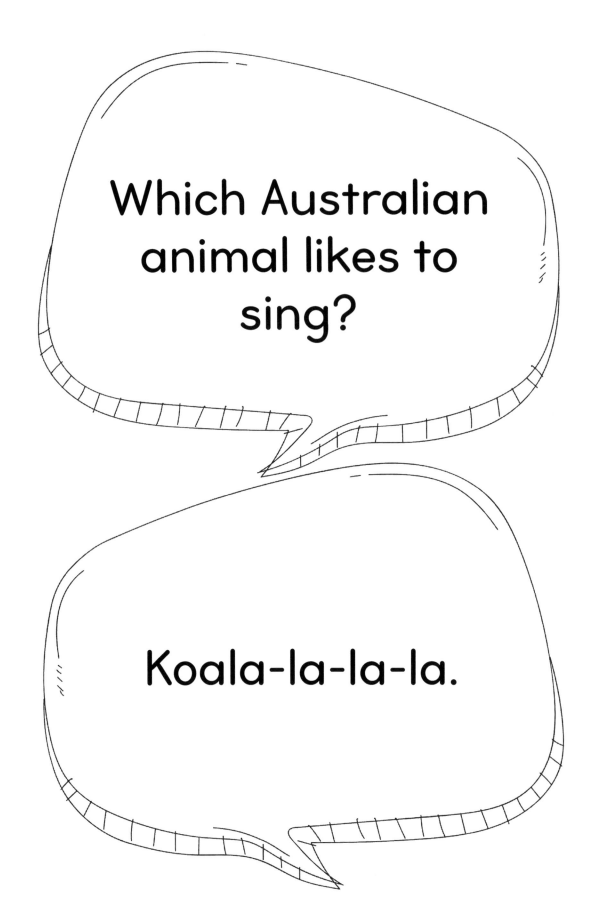

How many?

What are the two oldest animals on earth?

The zebra and the panda. Because they make them in black and white.

How many?

What public transport does a hippo use?

A hippopotabus.

How many?

Handwriting Practice

What time is it when a hippo, lion, and alligator are chasing you?

3 after 1.

Handwriting Practice

79

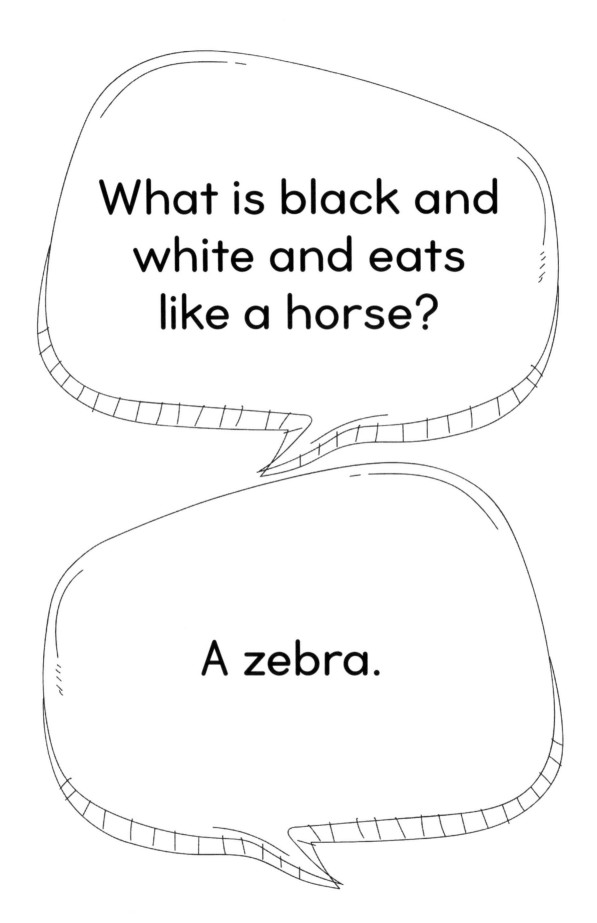

Handwriting Practice

Why did the elephant leave the circus?

Because he was tired of working for peanuts.

Dot to Dot

83

Which side of a leopard has more spots?

The outside.

Dot to Dot

85

Is it better to have a lion or a tiger eat you?

It's better that the lion eat the tiger.

Dot to Dot

87

How do monkeys get down the stairs?

They slide down the banana-ster!

Dot to Dot

What do you call an alligator that wears a vest?

An investigator.

Dot to Dot

91

Why did the hippo cross the road?

It was the chicken's day off.

Dot to Dot

How does a tiger greet other animals in the jungle?

Pleased to eat you.

Dot to Dot

95

What do sloths make when it snows?

Slow angels.

Dot to Dot

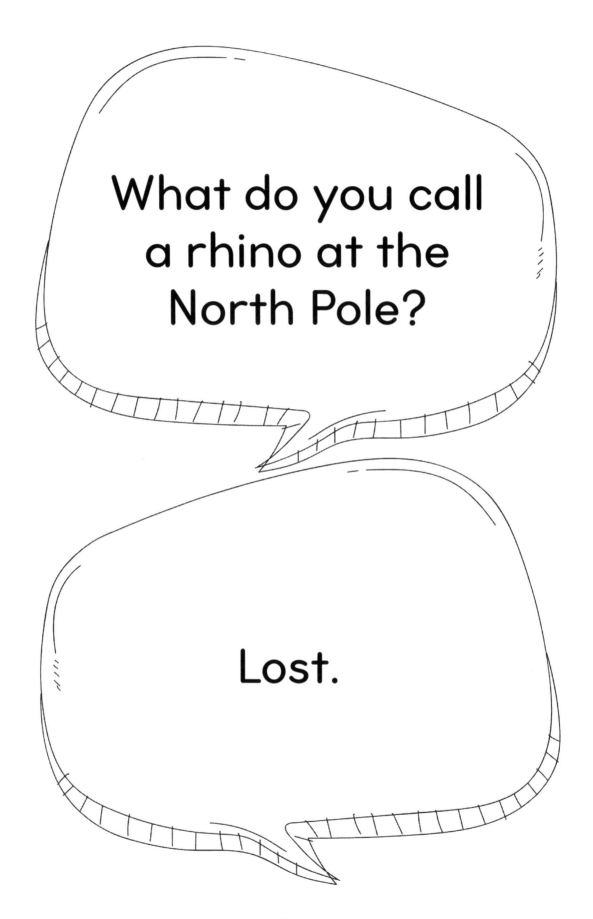

Dot to Dot

99

What do you call it when a giraffe swallows a toy jet?

A plane in the neck.

Dot to Dot

What is the difference between a zebra and a horse?

A zebra has his pajamas on.

Dot to Dot

Dot to Dot

105

LILY SILLY JOKES FOR KIDS
MUSIC INSTRUMENTS ACTIVITY FUN

AWESOME JOKES FOR 7-10 YEAR OLDS

Made in the USA
Columbia, SC
19 October 2020